BIBLE STORIES
FOR GIRLS

Retold by Christina Goodings
Illustrated by Simona Bursi

LION
CHILDREN'S

TO FLORA   S.B.

Text by Christina Goodings
Illustrations copyright © 2014 Simona Bursi
This edition copyright © 2014 Lion Hudson

Published by Lion Children's Books
an imprint of
Lion Hudson plc
Wilkinson House, Jordan Hill Road,
Oxford OX2 8DR, England
www.lionhudson.com/lionchildrens

ISBN 978 0 7459 6371 6

First edition 2014

A catalogue record for this book is available from the British Library

Printed and bound in China, November 2013, LH06

CONTENTS

BRAVE MIRIAM

THE STORY OF MIRIAM AND BABY MOSES

Being good isn't about meekly giving in; it's about having the courage to do what is right.

T HE KNOCK AT the door was followed by a shout.

"By order of the pharaoh, we demand you hand over the child!"

"It's them," shrilled the mother, in a frantic whisper. In one swift move, her daughter Miriam grabbed her baby brother from his hammock, put him on the floor, upended a vegetable basket over him, and sat on it.

The soldiers tramped in. "We are told you have a baby boy," said the officer. "The pharaoh's orders are that baby boys are to be thrown into the river. We have come to take him."

"Baby boy?" said Miriam, looking as little-girlish as she could.

"Who said that?" asked her mother.

Silently, both were praying that the baby wouldn't make any noise. Not now.

The officer glared around the room. He sent his men to prowl the other rooms. They returned having found nothing more interesting than the freshly baked bread that they were eating.

"It was worth coming for this," said the officer. Then he and his men left.

The mother dissolved into tears, but Miriam just looked fierce. "We must always be sure to have a large basket to hand," she said, as she stood up and uncovered her brother.

"We can't do that for ever!" wept her mother. "Your brother is growing. We can't keep him from the river for ever. I'd rather throw him in myself than have those soldiers take him."

Something pinged in Miriam's head. "We could make a bigger basket," she said, "like a boat – then we could float him in the river. If the soldiers come looking, you can truthfully say you put him in the river yourself."

"That would never work," her mother snapped. "Or would it?"

Suddenly Miriam was giggling. "Come on, let's fetch some reeds and begin making a cradle boat at once!"

The soldiers who came past the houses every day didn't take any notice of the mother and daughter coiling a large basket. It was much like any other. Painting it with tar wasn't odd either. A waterproof basket was useful for all sorts of things.

Like carrying washing down to the river. A mother and

daughter carrying a basket piled high with dirty linen was the most normal thing in the world.

And by that ruse, not long after, Miriam helped her mother carry her baby brother down to the river. They hid him at the most secret place they could think of in the reeds and rushes. Miriam stayed to watch that no harm came.

Oh no! Someone was coming. Lots of people. Miriam shuddered and made herself as small as possible. Worse – it was an Egyptian princess. With her servants. *They had chosen this very place to bathe in the river!*

Now the princess was checking around to make sure their secret bathing place was still undiscovered. That's how she saw the basket.

"Ooh, I wonder what that is," she said. "Can you fetch it for me, please?"

A maid waded into the water. She took the basket over to the princess. Together they lifted the lid.

"A baby!" squealed the princess. "Oh, the poor thing. Some poor mother who couldn't cope, I suppose."

Miriam watched with rising jealousy as the princess picked up her baby brother.

9

"I'm going to keep him," said the princess. "I'm going to call him Moses.

"But who could look after him for me?"

For the second time, something pinged in Miriam's head. She crept out of her hiding place and tiptoed up.

"Do you need someone to look after that baby?" she asked. "I know someone really good."

"Oh, please," said the princess.

Miriam brought her mother. The princess looked in turn at the baby, the mother, and the little girl. She gave a very big smile.

"I think we have the perfect arrangement," she said.

Victorious Women

The story of Deborah and the struggle for Canaan

Ah, Bible times. Women took traditional roles. They stayed at home and did cooking and sewing while their menfolk performed great and heroic deeds. Well, sometimes maybe. Not always.

WHEN JOSHUA LED the people of Israel into the land of Canaan, they believed it was their God-given home.

But the people were not faithful to their God. So God let their enemies come and challenge their claim.

There was a time when the Canaanite king Jabin launched one attack after another on the people of Israel. They became so desperate, they cried out to God to help them.

Now, among the leaders of the people was a wise woman named Deborah. There was a particular place where she would go and sit under a palm tree. People would come to ask for her

11

advice. Whatever she said was highly respected.

One day, she sent for a young warrior named Barak. "As you know, I speak on behalf of God," she said. "You are to summon fighting men and go and defeat the army of King Jabin."

Barak frowned. He was tempted to scoff and call Deborah "Granny". Happily he had been brought up to have better manners. So he tried to look very thoughtful indeed as he racked his brains for a way out of the job.

"I think it would be wrong for me to go without you," he said. That little ruse, he hoped, would put an end to the idea.

Deborah gave him a look that reminded Barak even more of his own granny. It was not a comfortable feeling.

"I'll come," she said. "But you won't be the hero of the action. A woman will claim the victory."

Barak shrugged. He couldn't see Deborah being much of a fighter. To his credit, he put some effort into calling up a huge army of fighting men. They set off to do battle.

Sisera, the commander of King Jabin's army, had been kept informed of every move. He called up the fighting men and nine hundred of the most up-to-date war chariots. He lined his forces up on the flat land near the River Kishon. From a high vantage point, Deborah surveyed the scene. Barak was at her side, trying to explain that Sisera's army looked very strong. Avoiding a fight might be better than suffering a defeat.

"Anyway, it looks like rain," he said, with hope in his voice. "I hear it's been wet in the hills for weeks."

Deborah glared. "Go," she said. "Fight Sisera's army today."

To be fair, Barak was very good at organizing his troops. "Oh well," he sighed to his best warriors. "Battle it must be. We might as well give the enemy a memorably blood-curdling battle cry."

At a signal, the army howled and whooped. Down by the river, Sisera's army leaped into action.

Then it began to rain. Rain in great heavy drops. Rain like twisted silver wire. Rain like the floodgates of heaven had opened.

The river rose. Barak saw a great crest of water rolling down from the mountains. It swept over the plain and the nine hundred heavy chariots sunk into the mud.

Barak was delighted. The enemy were on the run. "Come on!" he shouted. "Let's finish them off."

Sisera himself escaped the battlefield. He ran into the hill country; then he plodded. By the time evening came, he was barely stumbling along.

"Phew," he said. "I see a tent. An encampment. Can't be Israelites, they're not nomads. Maybe they'll help."

A woman named Jael greeted him. "Come into the tent," she said. "I won't let anyone search in here."

Then she brought Sisera some milk.

The weary fighter drank deeply. Then he curled up on a rug. "If anyone comes asking, say that you've seen no one," he pleaded.

Jael nodded. She watched the man fall asleep. Then she picked up a tent peg and a hammer. She looked at Sisera's head. And then she did the deed that sealed the victory.

Some time later, Barak came by. Jael called out to him.

"If you're wanting Sisera," she said, "his body is here."

Naomi Looks Back

THE STORY OF NAOMI AND RUTH

Sometimes things in life go well; sometimes they go not so well. Badly, even. But those who go on doing what is right and good may see things change again.

IF ANYONE HAD asked Naomi, "What was the best moment in your life?" she knew what she would say.

It was when she had her first child, a boy. She could recall the moment in detail. She was sitting in the house, the child neatly swathed in a blanket she had made with her own hands. Her husband had come running to see his son, but was outrun by her own mother. Suddenly all three grown-ups were laughing with joy, and the infant made a face very like a smile. And the memory always made Naomi smile too.

As for the worst moment: there were too many, and she didn't

care to think about them. Things began to go wrong after her second child was born. The weather had been poor and the harvest failed. Her husband had decided to take his family to a new land, Moab, and build a new life there.

Naomi had missed her old home in Bethlehem and the support of her friends and relatives. But at least they could make a living in Moab. Then her husband had died.

Naomi could not help but be sad; but she was a mother and she had to keep the family going. Her two boys had grown up strong and handsome. They had both married Moabite girls – lovely girls, whom Naomi really liked. Then both sons had died. Naomi had felt more alone than ever.

At last there had come what sounded like good news. Back in Bethlehem, the years of poor weather were over. The harvests were excellent. Naomi made a plan: she would go back home.

She had set off with her two daughters-in-law: they had become part of her household when they married. As they walked along, Naomi had begun to worry. How would she look after them? Would they feel at home? Suddenly, the future had

seemed full of problems.

She had stopped right there in the road: "It's not right for you to come with me," she had said. "Please go back to your old family homes. You are still young and could marry again, among your own people."

Both women had been reduced to tears at what Naomi was asking. However, after much talking one agreed to go. The other, Ruth, had wept and pleaded to be allowed to come.

"I want to be with you," she had said. "I want to be accepted as one of your people. I want to follow your traditions, and worship your God."

Naomi had finally agreed. After a long journey the two women had arrived in Bethlehem.

Naomi's old friends had been astonished. "Naomi!" they had exclaimed. "After all these years! Tell us your news."

Naomi had blinked back her tears. "It's all bad news, really," she said. "It's left me feeling really bitter."

Ruth had been determined to do what was right. "You've told me that it's the custom here for the poor to glean the leftover harvest," she had said. "Let me go gleaning so that we have something to eat."

As she worked in the fields, the farmer saw the young woman and asked about her. When he found out, he gave his workers this instruction:

"She is such a good daughter-in-law. Let her collect all she needs. Make sure there's plenty spare for her.

"And remember to let her share in the food I've provided for you."

That day had surely been the turning point. Naomi did just a little scheming to make sure Boaz didn't think of Ruth as just "the foreign girl"… and her plan worked. With one very clear result:

To the delight of everyone in Bethlehem, Boaz asked Ruth to marry him.

It wasn't long after that Naomi had the equal best moment in her life.

There was Ruth, cuddling her newborn baby – a boy, wrapped in the blanket Naomi had made with her own hands. Boaz was running to see his son; but Naomi outran him.

And then they all laughed together.

BEAUTY QUEEN

THE STORY OF ESTHER

*Is it a good thing to be famous? Does it depend on what
you're famous for? Is beauty enough?*

THE SERVANT GIRL held up the mirror so that Esther could gaze at
her reflection: the Persian queen. And she sighed.

As a little girl, she'd dreamed of a life less ordinary. Her uncle
Mordecai, who had brought her up, had been so *serious*. He'd just
wanted her to grow up a good Jewish girl, faithful to her God and
her people's traditions.

She'd wanted clothes and make-up and the fun of having lots
of parties. Then, as a young woman, she'd entered a contest to be
the next queen. *And she'd won.* She'd won because she was slender

and pretty and looked fabulous whatever she chose to wear: a plain linen tunic, a jewel-encrusted gown, harem pants and a silky top… everything looked good on her.

It was for her looks that the king had chosen Esther. But now her uncle – no, all the Jews in the empire – needed her to appeal to the king on a serious matter.

It wasn't her place to make a request. It was against the law even for her to go to the king without being summoned. Some people who'd done that had been put to death for their impertinence.

"Pray for me," she said to her servant girls, and she set off toward the throne room.

Esther stood just outside, trembling with fear. The king saw his young wife and frowned ever so slightly. She didn't belong in the working part of the palace. When had he last made time to see her in the evening? Too long, perhaps. Slowly the king raised his golden sceptre. It was the sign that Esther was being invited to approach him.

"What have you come for, Queen Esther?" he asked. "I promise that you'll have it."

"Simply to invite you to a banquet," she replied. "You and your chief advisor, Haman."

"How nice!" replied the king. He felt rather pleased that he had chosen such a brave and respectful wife. And Haman was always good fun: waspish, perhaps, but witty.

Esther planned for everything about the banquet to be perfect, and the evening went very well.

"Now," said the king, as he set down his wineglass. "What's this

22

all for? What are you wanting?"

Esther smiled. "If you would be so kind as to come to another banquet tomorrow as well, then I will ask."

So the banquet ended. Haman went home well pleased with himself.

"My invitation to the queen's private banquet is proof that I have been accepted right at the heart of the palace," he told his wife.

And as he was that important, he surely had the right to get rid of his arch-enemy, a Jew named Mordecai.

"I'll have a gallows built to hang him on," he said.

That would be one Jew fewer. There wasn't long to go until the day he'd agreed with the king for all the Jews in the empire to be exterminated.

The following day, however, brought Haman bad news. Out of the blue, the king had discovered some dutiful act Mordecai had done ages before. Now he wanted him rewarded for his service. And he asked Haman to organize a public parade for the Jew. Even as he did the king's bidding, he was thinking of how little time there was until he would get final revenge on Mordecai and all his people.

Haman was relieved when the sun set and it was time to go to the second banquet. Esther had arranged another perfect evening: the décor, the food, the wine… simply fabulous.

"And now, Queen Esther," said the king. "What is it you want?"

23

"Your Majesty," replied Esther, gravely. "I want to be allowed to live – I and all my people. We have learned of a plan to have us all killed."

"That's outrageous," said the king. "Who is behind this wicked plan?"

"Our enemy," replied Esther icily, "is that evil man there: Haman."

The king was so angry at the news that he simply walked out of the room and stormed around the gardens.

He returned to find Haman clutching at Esther and pleading with her.

"LET GO OF MY WIFE!" he roared.

One of the servants stepped forward. "You may find it useful to know," he said, "that within the past day Haman had a gallows built on which to hang the loyal Jew Mordecai."

"Did he?" said the king. "Then Haman himself shall have full use of the gallows."

And so Haman's plan was overturned. Queen Esther and Mordecai together became famous for defending the Jews: their faith and their traditions.

THE TWO SISTERS

THE STORY OF MARY AND MARTHA

Every day is filled with things that keep a person busy; but what are the important things to do?

MARTHA WAS SITTING on the flat rooftop in the cool shade of a vine. She paused from her darning. Below, in the courtyard, her brother Lazarus and her sister Mary were laughing as they worked. Lazarus was on a ladder among the branches of their fig tree. Mary was catching the fruit he threw and laying it on a wicker tray. She had already filled several trays and carried them to the rooftop so that the fruit could dry in the sun. Martha smiled. Life was good.

How things had changed over the last little while. Martha remembered the difficult days, when she found herself alone in charge of the household. Lazarus had never been strong and she

25

was worried every time he fell ill. Mary was sweet, but such a dreamer. Had Martha been wrong to call her a lazybones in those days? When Martha felt she was doing all the work to keep the family together?

Martha remembered the day they had invited Jesus to come and share a meal with them. It was Mary's idea. She was the one who had gone off to join the crowds who listened to his teaching. She had been the one to tell his friends that if they needed a place to stay in Bethany then they would be welcome at her home. And they'd said yes, please. What a day it had been – preparing a meal and everything for thirteen men.

Martha had tidied and swept and baked and stirred all day. Mary had twittered on about how excited she was. Oh, and she'd filled jugs with wild flowers to make the humble home "smell nice".

And then, when the visitors arrived, Mary had simply sat down to listen to everything Jesus said.

That's when Martha had lost her temper. "Tell that lazybones to come and help me," she'd shouted at Jesus.

She felt ashamed of that outburst now. She remembered how foolish she'd felt when Jesus replied, "You are busy with so many things, but Mary has chosen to do the most important thing of all."

Back in the kitchen she had wept. Then she did the one thing she was good at: she had served the meal and everyone had to agree the food was very, very good.

Later, when she too was listening to Jesus, she knew he hadn't wanted to make her feel bad.

In fact, the way he put things seemed chosen especially to thank her for all her hard work.

"My message is about being part of God's kingdom," he'd said. "The kingdom of heaven is like this: a woman loses a coin in her house. She lights a lamp and sweeps into every dark corner until she finds it. When she finds it, she is overjoyed and calls her neighbours around to celebrate.

"In the same way, God celebrates over every person who turns their life around to live as one of God's family.

"And here's another way to think of the kingdom. A woman takes a pinch of yeast and mixes it into a bowlful of flour. The yeast makes the whole batch of dough rise."

From that point, Martha too began to hang on Jesus' words. God's kingdom sounded like the place she wanted to be: a place of love and goodness.

Mary had been affected too. She must surely have noticed Jesus' choice of words. After he'd gone, Mary had changed from being the one who somehow dodged the household chores into the one who got up early to begin them. The kingdom wasn't just about fine words any more, but hard-working deeds as well.

That was when both sisters really put their trust in Jesus and his teaching. They believed the stories of how he healed people. And when Lazarus fell ill, they both agreed that if anyone could save him, it was Jesus.

They'd sent a message. While they waited, Lazarus had died.
They'd had the funeral and everything.

Then Jesus arrived. Mary was lost in grief. Martha still believed
that Jesus could help.

And he had. He'd told the people of Bethany to open the tomb.
He'd called to Lazarus — and Lazarus had walked back from death
to life.

Now Lazarus was well. Now the household was full of goodness
and love, of laughter and happiness.

A little piece of the kingdom, really. Martha put down her
darning. "I would rather go and smell the flowers," she said.

THE WOMAN WHO KNEW SHE WAS RIGHT

If you really believe in something, you'll work hard to make it happen. Jesus explained that those who pray to God for help must be patient and never give up. He told a story of a widow and a judge to show that not giving up works even on the meanest of human beings.

R EUBEN WAS WALKING as fast as he could. That wasn't very fast, as he was rather stout. In fact, he was getting rather puffed as he tried to escape the person following him.

Then he saw someone he knew: the Roman centurion in charge of the troops who policed the town.

"Marcus," he cried. "How lovely to see you. I was just wondering if I might have a quick word with you about the little

30

incident involving a brawl between…"

And with that he hustled Marcus toward the centurion's house, which was a lot closer than Reuben's own.

That clever move stopped the person behind catching up with him. A judge, such as Reuben was, could easily think of some matter of law and order he could usefully discuss with the centurion. Anyway, Marcus was almost a friend.

"I actually had something to talk about with you," said Marcus, when they were safely inside. "Hiram does a wonderful job around here collecting taxes for the emperor. I hear he's having a bit of bother with some old woman. She's claiming he's stolen part of her vegetable garden."

"Don't I know it!" exclaimed Reuben. "I've just been dealing with her case. Not for the first time. She insists the stones that mark the edge of her garden have been moved. Says she remembers learning from her own grandmother how they all lined up with the sun's shadow at noon or some nonsense. If there is a distance, it's a matter of a few paces."

"Indeed," said Marcus, snapping his fingers toward a servant and indicating he wanted refreshments brought. "And yet," he added, leaning forward, "for Hiram, a critical few paces, if he is to build his new mansion to the design he wants."

After an hour or so of talking and a nice glass of wine, Reuben set off for home.

Oh no! There was the nagging old… he couldn't think of a word bad enough to describe the woman. Would she never give up?

31

"Please, sir," the old woman was saying. "I have friends who have agreed to come and give evidence about my case. They not only know where the marker stones should be, their son remembers seeing some men moving them. He remembers the day exactly."

"Hearsay," replied the judge, "from people who are already on your side. Dishonest people, I might add. I know that Hiram is having to chase several of them to pay the tax he has calculated they owe."

He marched off home, feeling smug. He enjoyed a lovely meal and spent the evening watering his flower garden. He fell asleep very content.

The new day brought work as usual. Reuben sighed mildly as he strode past the line of people with arguments to settle who were eager to see him.

Oh dear – she'd come again. When the woman stepped forward with a couple of friends either side, Reuben raised his eyes to the ceiling. He couldn't stand the sound of her voice. Always ever-so-humble yet ever so unstoppable.

But now she was getting a bit agitated. That was good. It gave Reuben the excuse he needed to ask one of the police guards to lead her away. No one is allowed to get disorderly when dealing with matters of law. That got rid of her.

Until the next day. Oh… please… no.

The woman was back. She was driving him crazy.

And anyway, everyone knew the rights and wrongs of her case. Everyone who had lived in the town since before Hiram had been brought in to collect the emperor's taxes. Never mind Marcus and his fine wines. Never mind Hiram and his grand design.

Reuben beckoned to his scribe and had a quiet word with him. The man went and wrote as quickly as he could on several sheets of parchment.

Reuben gave one to a guard, two to a court messenger, and one to the woman.

"Please go home," he said. "I've asked the guard to arrange for men to come and move the stones to where you say they were. You will not be hearing from Hiram and you are not to speak to him."

"Thank you, sir," replied the old woman. "God bless you."

How to Be a Bridesmaid

JESUS' PARABLE OF THE WISE AND FOOLISH BRIDESMAIDS

One day, Jesus said, God will come to this world in power and glory. He will gather into his kingdom those who are faithful and obedient. No one knows when that will happen. It is important always to be ready. Jesus told a story about ten bridesmaids.

JUDITH WAS THE eldest of the bridesmaids and she was getting quite bothered. The bridegroom was due to arrive any minute, but the other bridesmaids were bickering and fretting about the tiniest things.

"Oh do stop FUSSING and just make sure you're READY!" she hissed at the other nine girls.

"But my head wreath is coming apart," complained Suzy. "I just asked Rebekah to put back a flower that had fallen out but whatever she did has made it worse."

35

"I didn't make it worse. It was already falling apart," argued Rebekah.

"I don't know what to do about my hem," moaned Abigail. "I caught my sandal in it and now it's coming down."

"I brought a needle," exclaimed Joanna. There was a note of triumph in her voice. "Let me see where I need to put a stitch."

Sometimes Joanna was annoying in the way she thought of everything, but right now Judith was relieved.

"Alright, Joanna." she said, "Go stitch.

"Rebekah: I'm sure you did your best but whatever it was hasn't worked.

"Lizzie: can you run over to the field and pick a few more daisies? Then, Suzy, I will use them to fix your head wreath.

"Debs: we need to light our lamps. You go inside to light yours, and then everyone can light their lamp from yours."

Apart from the fact that Rebekah, Cilla, Eunice, Abigail, and Mary all trooped into the house with Debs, everything went to plan. It fact, because all six came out with their lamps burning merrily, it was very quick to get everyone's lamp lit.

"Now we want five of us one side of the path and five the other. Suzy and Rebekah, opposite sides for you two and DON'T make faces at each other!

"Right. Now we wait."

And so the ten girls waited. The sun slipped behind the horizon. Ten little lamps twinkled merrily in the dark.

But there was no sign of the bridegroom. First Rebekah let out

a sigh and put her lamp down. Beside her Cilla, Eunice, Mary, and Abigail did the same. Then Rebekah rummaged in her waist bag and pulled out a bottle of perfume. She made a big show of putting some on. Then she let Cilla, Eunice, Mary, and Abigail all have some, but nobody else. Next Rebekah smirked at Suzy and put the bottle away. Suzy yawned and let her head slump onto Judith's shoulder.

"Sit up, or you'll crush your head wreath," Judith whispered. Suzy sprung back up. Then she too put her lamp on the ground and sat down with her back to a wall. She took off her head wreath and laid it in her lap.

Rebekah, Cilla, Eunice, Mary, and Abigail exchanged glances. As if in secret agreement they also took off their head wreaths.

Then they slumped into one another and closed their eyes. Joanna, Debs, and Lizzie shuffled back to the wall to rest their heads. Judith remained standing for quite a while. When she heard the owls hooting, she too sat down.

By her side, Suzy was slumped against Lizzie, eyes closed, fast asleep.

In fact, everyone was asleep. Judith felt her eyelids drooping. No, she mustn't be caught napping. It was her friend's wedding, after all.

All of a sudden, cheers rang out. "Here comes the bridegroom! Everyone come and greet him."

The bridesmaids leaped to their feet.

"Oh, look at the flames — they've burned low," gasped Judith. "Gather around — I'll trim the wicks to make them burn brighter.

"Suzy, your lamp is almost empty."

"I've got more oil," said Suzy. She rummaged in her bag. "I put it in an old perfume bottle. And the one you asked me to look after, Judith."

"I've got some oil too," said Joanna. Debs and Lizzie were already refilling their lamps while they waited their turn to trim the wicks.

"I hope you lot are going to share," said Rebekah haughtily.

"You are joking, aren't you?" said Judith. "I told you all we might need more oil."

"She did," said Joanna. "When we were making the head wreaths."

"I just forgot," wailed Cilla.

"Then just go and get some RIGHT NOW!" Judith was almost shouting. "Listen: can you hear the band? That means the procession is COMING! So go and get some oil sharpish."

Rebekah, Cilla, Eunice, Abigail, and Mary ran off, bleating about selfish meanies.

They returned to the sounds of a party in full swing. And the sight of a locked door.

"Lift me up to the window," whispered Rebekah. "I'll shout to someone to let us in."

Below the other four heard her pleading. But no one inside was taking any notice. No one came to the door.

Finally Rebekah dropped down.

"I hate that bridegroom," she said. "He made it quite clear he's not letting anyone else in.

"Ooh, look." She gave an unkind laugh. "There's Suzy's head wreath. Won't she look a disaster."

Cilla kicked the limp flowers. "I don't suppose she cares," she said.

"At least she's AT the party," complained Eunice.

"Unlike us," added Abigail.

"And I didn't even want your stupid perfume, Rebekah," said Mary. Then she burst into tears.

Lydia Means Business

Lydia and the early church in Philippi

People who have money and influence can choose how to spend their time. But the choices aren't always easy.

LYDIA COULD HARDLY believe what her secretary was telling her. Nor was she pleased.

"You say that Susannah has come to visit when she knows I'm working?" Lydia was sitting at her desk, pen in hand.

"I'm afraid so, Madam," replied the secretary. "I did remind her, but she said she knew. She pointed out that your business has made you wealthy, and that a wealthy woman can take time off when she likes."

"My business has made me wealthy because I don't take time off willy-nilly," replied Lydia.

"Right now a whole shipload of purple cloth is stuck at the

dockside while some petty official fusses about taxes on luxury imports. As if I don't know more than he does about luxury imports. I've been in the purple cloth business for years. I have to get a message taken down at once to sort it all out.

"Ask Susannah to wait in the gardens until I'm free."

A voice boomed from the next room. "Halloo there, Lydia darling!"

It was too late. Susannah had breezed in unbidden. Lydia glared.

"I know what you're thinking," gushed Susannah.

To be fair, she probably did. Susannah and Lydia had known each other for years. Decent, God-fearing women who went to the same prayer meeting each sabbath. They had different lifestyles, but there was more they agreed on than they argued about.

"I know you'll think this is important," announced Susannah. "That curious preacher Paul who came and spoke at our prayer meeting – he's in trouble."

"Oh no!" Both Lydia and her secretary looked alarmed.

Paul and his friends had arrived at their sabbath meeting and preached about a new way of seeing their faith: the way that someone named Jesus had taught. Lydia had been utterly convinced. She had been baptized as a sign of her belief. Her home had become a meeting place for believers — Followers of the Way, they were sometimes called. Paul and his friends were Lydia's guests.

"It's absolute mayhem in town," continued Susannah. "You know Paul cured the fortune-telling girl of her crazy ranting. Well, her owners are furious. She doesn't do the soothsaying anymore and so they make no money. They had Paul and Silas publicly arrested for preaching things that are "un-Roman". The crowd were baying for blood. So the town clerk had Paul and Silas whipped and then thrown into jail."

Lydia gasped. She picked up her pen and a fresh piece of papyrus. "I shall send a message at once to those nincompoops at the town hall," she said.

"Or," said Susannah, leaning forward, "you might like to think hard about your new enthusiasm. Maybe you shouldn't put your trust in Paul's message. Our faith, our customs, our traditions — weren't they fine before Paul?"

Lydia wrote swiftly and handed the folded message to her secretary, who left with it at once.

Lydia fixed Susannah with a sharp look. "Our faith, our customs, and our traditions were fine," she said crisply, "but what Paul has told us about Jesus just brings them all to life. It's a way of seeing things that is more loving, more forgiving, and includes all sorts and conditions of people, Jews and Greeks, slaves and citizens – probably even those nincompoops at the town hall and a particularly petty official down at the port.

"And now, Susannah, thank you *so* much for bringing me the news, but I really must get back to work."

Except that work didn't seem so important. Two friends were in big trouble. She and Susannah were clearly in one of their "at loggerheads" phases. But then again, it was a huge amount of purple cloth that was being held up at the port. Oh dear.

Lydia finished her work and then went to her room to say a prayer asking God to take care of Paul and Silas. Even so, she couldn't sleep that night. Around midnight the house shook – another earth tremor, she supposed.

Then in the morning she got ready to go to the town hall and have Paul and Silas released.

She was hurrying along the road when they called a greeting.

"You're free!" exclaimed Lydia, as Paul and Silas approached. "How did you get out?"

"Well, there was a small earthquake last night," said Silas. "It broke the doors open. Not that there was any trouble because of that. It simply gave us the chance to do some preaching in the prison. Mainly to the jailer."

"And this morning I had the chance to remind the nincompoops who arrived from the town hall that I'm a Roman citizen," said Paul. "I pointed out that whipping us and flinging us in jail was not only wrong but illegal. All of a sudden they turned very humble indeed."

Lydia let out a sigh of relief. "Well, I did send a message to plead your case," she said, "but it seems that my prayers may have done more."

So that was job number one sorted already. Now, which task next: sorting the purple cloth or sending a friendly note to Susannah?